I0191633

CONCRETE'S SONG

Copyright © 2018 Lloyd David Aquino
All rights reserved. No part of this book may be used or
reproduced in any manner whatsoever without written
permission from the author, except in the case of credited
epigraphs or brief quotations embedded in articles or reviews.

Acknowledgments: "Hector who cuts hair in quiet Spanish"
was first published by *Blue Earth Review*. "Jenny who will stay"
was originally published as "Jenny who won't leave" by *MUSE
Magazine*. "Amna with stars spinning around her" was first
published by *Carnival*. "Shannon with tattoos all around her
neck" was first published in the chapbook *Madeline After the Fall*
by Arroyo Seco Press.

www.pictureshowpress.net

Cover image: Floriana, istockphoto.com

FIRST EDITION

ISBN-13: 978-1-7324144-1-9
ISBN-10: 1-7324144-1-6

Concrete's Song

Lloyd David Aquino

Picture Show Press

For all those who
ought to have poetry
written about them

Poems

In the kitchen, she doesn't cook, she sings
to the grandson in the crook of her arm,

A-po-po-ching, a-po-po-ching, making
up her song while she nuzzles his red cheek

dimpled with laughter. Shuffling on slippers,
she sings, *A-ching-ching-ching, a-pwet-pwet-ching,*

scuffling the tile to wake the labradors
and dachshunds her daughter asked her to keep,

four sets of ears that perk up at each name
she adds to her song. She claps in rhythm

to the legs and tails dancing around her,
then needs three tries to shush the room, to sit

and answer the phone, to calm the caller
with a chorus of *Uh-huh, oh, oh-ho.*

Rachel with the Good Hair! Rachel the Brown!
Rachel Who Will Not Be Having Any
Today! Rachel with the Bionic Knees!
Rachel the Bowlegged! Rachel the Girl
Who Stuck the Stars to Her Ceiling Because
She Could! Rachel of the Leopards! Rachel
of the Mustangs! Rachel, No, Not Raquel!
Rachel Who Suffered Pink Slips and Survived!
Rachel Who Gave Birth Eleven Weeks Too
Soon and, Yes, Survived! Rachel the Patient!
Rachel Who Drifts across Wet Parking Lots!
Rachel, Devourer of Meats and Cheese
and Ice Creams! Rachel, Mother of Two Sons!
Rachel the Wiser! Rachel! Friend! Sister!

There's a monster gurgling in the shallows
who loves him, who hungers for toes wriggling

like fish caught on hooks. Mouth full of baby
teeth, the boy splashes tidal wave after

wave, bubbling with laughter, childish laughter
that loves whatever it touches, laughter

the monster longs to hear again, would drown
and drown to hear again. The boy lingers,

his brown hair alight like Oahu sun.
Bubbles like claws crawl forward. The boy kicks

to break the surface of restless water.
The monster is sent floating on its back,

eyelids red, lips pulled over crooked teeth.
Leaping, the boy pulls the sun down with him.

Hector who cuts hair in quiet Spanish
moves to the static of his *novelas,*

brushes away piles with his broom inside
pale, green walls. Every chair empty but one,

the clippers drawling, the cushions sharing
weekend plans for family barbeques.

Hector whose spectacles don't see the sun
works beside a black-lettered sign that says

Se vende la barberia, lathers
foam to slather across beards beckoning

straight razors, strokes chins with precise, bloodless
cuts. His quiet Spanish settles black combs

untangling unruly heads while he laughs
and gives little boys their fathers' haircuts.

Dig a hole in the dirt. Do not worry
the splinters. The persimmon tree's snapped trunk

might survive a drought. Ripe papayas will
fall. Now go dig more holes. Wet soil layers

cracked palms that have grown since he was a boy
in Dumaguete. He climbed coconut

trees. He dove so deep light could not follow.
Now the dogs chase after the garden hose

among the winter grass. Wind rattles bare
branches. He climbs, handsaw in hand. Darkness

swallows the sky. Now quiet dogs watch him
cut down limb after limb. Sawdust dapples

the sweat that patters the dirt. A moonlit
silhouette stands where a dead tree once stood.

Kanani who sways to island music
sits in the garden shade and teaches boys

to roust awkward limbs, to shake them into
the shape of ancient gods, forest giants

with waterfalls for arms. In her yellow-
flowered, blue-skinned sundress, she says, *Loosen.*

You're too stiff, like bamboo. Now try again.
Kanani who limps to the tilt of her

straw hat straightens pigeon toes to *knock-knock*
floorboards, unfolds shy fingers to conjure

cranes like origami idle boys fold
and puff up with puffed cheeks to flood the sky

with paper. *When you dance,* she pronounces,
every step should summon home the ocean.

Manuel with muscles and a green tank top
moves fingers that motion blur so eyelids

stutter open and shut, that juke inside
and out of notes flung from the nest of strings

on his guitar, notes that hatch black-winged birds
with beaks burning to gulp down breathless breaths.

Manuel who sings in dynamite couplets
exploding against concrete-colored walls,

echoing off chairs, vibrates through clothing,
through flesh, until every vein *twangs* in tune.

Manuel who cracks Fret House stairs to kindling
crosses Citrus Avenue, a sweat-soaked

tank top and a guitar case in one hand,
and finds a storefront where he can still play.

Yessenia behind the register
takes the hundred pound bill, makes change. There's rain

in her hair, jangling like coins in a fist.
She asks about California palm trees.

Do they speak Spanish? In Colombia,
they sing all day and night. She doesn't wait

for an answer. Shifting her weight, she wipes
down counters and smiles at her reflection.

In the back kitchen, chicken sizzles like
downpour on cobblestone streets. Pale faces

absorb light from palm-sized screens. Old bridges
along the Thames conceal people in grey.

Yessenia whose brown skin remembers
the sun counts the steps from here to the door.

Leslie whose daughter is turning thirty
says to the usher who checks their tickets

We'll take it from here, sugar, smile scented
apple cinnamon. The women dish out

stories of dollars and cents socked away
for a weekend on Broadway, a dinner

and a show. Onstage, a Southern waitress
gives birth to a baby girl, love-scented,

sends away broken men who care too much
about themselves. House lights brighten wet eyes.

Leslie who buys pies served in small glass jars
claps to the heartbeat of a show closer,

a curtain call. On West 47th,
she stops traffic to find her daughter's hand.

Jenny who will stay repeats the statement,
Phillip has a really good heart. Six days

since he pissed his mom's disability
checks away on video games. *He loves*

Aaron, their son, one of those boys who charms
his way into wherever he pleases,

who break-dances at weddings and horses
around coffee tables until bedtime.

He would never lay a finger on me,
No, never, never. No, he won't touch her

when he breaks because no one's hiring now,
it's never ever his fault. Jenny says,

No one can help who they fall in love with,
only her voice splinters after four words.

Sandra who will walk away buys us tea
and says, *Maybe love's not enough,* white scarf

hiding her neck. I let the cup go cold.
Her eyes follow the passing cars instead

of the words pouring out of me like smoke.
I bury myself in her hair, hold her

tightly until I can't. I forget how
to breathe. Children are laughing around us.

Often I think of the rain in Mammoth.
The silence of the trees and the murmur

of the slumbering lake. How we clamored
up rocks to talk to birds. How she held me

close and whispered, *You're the love of my life.*
How I kissed her warm lips and believed her.

Shannon with tattoos all around her neck,
flowers blooming from concrete of old scars

she speaks of in a poem, cracks the cracks
in the walls as she wraps one fist around

the microphone, steadies the aftershocks,
gasps the words *facial reconstruction*, rasps

how bones, like dreams, shatter upon impact,
how one accident doesn't mean we no

longer have choices, how the word *helpless*
is a fiction. Her neck has turned to fire

clawing for air when she stops at the last
period in the poem. The room claps

thunder to trap in jars, to uncork if
another car collision comes for her.

Amna with stars spinning around her says
she enjoys the sight of naked women,

orders whiskey instead of lemon drops.
Manhattanites speak eighties pop patois,

Do you really want to hurt me, baby,
'cause I'm hungry like a wolf, so don't you

forget about me. Giggling a tall glass
of Hefeweizen and a shot of Jack

to soak the bottom shelf of her stomach,
she reminisces about hangovers

that stuffed her head full of old furniture,
about street vendors making love-sick pleas.

Amna with stardust on her lips watches
city lights fall like meteor showers.

Charlie with paws that break dog biscuits makes
no sound as he rests on my chest. We drive

the 15 together, no radio,
learning how each other breathes. Charlie sniffs

at the words I whisper and repeat, warmth
pouring from his fur. Claws crumple my shirt.

Charlie with paws that engulf tennis balls
howls in his cage. He can't stand up straight, so

he jimmies the lock to escape, slashes
the living room rug and terrorizes

the toilet paper until I come home
to shake my head and to rub his belly.

Charlie with paws that flatten soccer balls
lies against my back, quiet as moonlight.

Lloyd David Aquino teaches composition, literature, and creative writing at Mount San Antonio College. His first poetry chapbook, *Madeline After the Fall,* is available through Arroyo Seco Press. He is currently working on his first novel, a western adventure titled *All the Worst Cheats.*

www.ingramcontent.com/pod-product-compliance
Lightning Source LLC
Chambersburg PA
CBHW020037040426
42331CB00031B/961